MW01635676

The Country Kitchen
JAMS &
MARMALADES
Barbara Beckett

The Country Kitchen
JAMS &
MARMALADES
Barbara Beckett

HARLAXTON
PUBLISHING

Front and back of jacket: The attractive results of a week's cooking. Left to right: rhubarb and orange jam (p.26), strawberry jam (p.26), orange marmalade (p.39), quince jelly (p.33), tomato jam (p.27), apricot jam (p.15) and a close-up of the texture of the orange marmalade.

Front and back endpapers: An old-fashioned country kitchen with the preparation for a spicy fruit cake in the foreground. The wood burning stove is wonderful for long, slow cooking.

Page 2: Lime marmalade is appetizing with cake and cream for brunch.

COOK'S NOTES: Standard spoon and cup measurements are used in all recipes.
All spoon measurements are level.

Some fruits can be frozen when brought or picked if it is not possible to make jams and marmalades immediately.

Published by Harlaxton Publishing Ltd
2 Avenue Road, Grantham, Lincolnshire, NG31 6TA, United Kingdom.
A Member of the Weldon International Group of Companies.

First published in 1992.
Reprinted in 1993.

© Copyright Harlaxton Publishing Ltd
© Copyright design Harlaxton Publishing Ltd

Publishing Manager: Robin Burgess
Project Coordinator: Barbara Beckett
Designer & Illustrator : Barbara Beckett
Photographer: Ray Jarratt
Editor in United Kingdom: Alison Leach
Typeset in United Kingdom: Seller's, Grantham
Produced in Singapore by Imago

All rights reserved.
No part of this publication may be reproduced,
stored in a retrieval system, or transmitted in any form or by any means,
electronic, mechanical, photocopying, recording, or otherwise,
without the prior written permission of the copyright owner.

British Library Cataloguing-in-Publication data.
A catalogue record for this book is available from the British Library.
Title: Country Kitchen Series: Jams & Marmalades
ISBN:1 85837 003 5

Contents

Old Fashioned
Marmalade
7/5

Introduction to Jam & Marmalade Making

IT REALLY isn't a lot of trouble to make jams and jellies once you have gained a little experience. I am inspired to make them whenever I see the various fruits come into season. The heaps of shining oranges, apples or plums immediately make me think of making orange marmalade, apple paste or plum and ginger jam. I love to preserve peaches and apricots and pears while they are cheap to buy so that my family and friends can enjoy them all the year round. Jams, jellies, conserves and pastes can also be turned into a dessert or a sauce for a meat dish.

It is very satisfying to eat something you have made yourself. What you've made will always be a finer quality than anything you could buy, and you will have saved money. A jar of homemade jam makes a thoughtful gift for a friend, too.

Throughout the recipes I have specified different quantities of fruit. Some are large amounts, for when there is a glut of that particular fruit. They will still work if you carefully halve the ingredients. Others are smaller and more manageable. Read 'Making Jam', right, before trying any of the recipes to avoid the dread of every jam maker-a failed set.

Old-fashioned marmalade made from Seville oranges. The two oranges in the foreground, with their greenish hue, are a perfect under-ripe condition, ideal for jam making.

COOK'S NOTES: Scrub the skins of fruit thoroughly before using, in order to remove any pesticides and the wax used to make the skins shiny.

MAKING JAM

A good jam is bright and clear and tastes of the original fruit. It should be set but not solid, and of course it should keep well. Total success in all these respects may not always be possible, because the quality of the fruit varies according to its sugar and water content and ripeness. Over-ripe fruit tends to lose flavor and pectin, which is what helps the jam to set. Even the size and shape of the saucepan can affect the rate of evaporation of the water. If you follow the basic guidelines in this introduction you should be able to avoid mishaps.

Fruit

Always wash or scrub the fruit carefully to remove any pesticides or wax.

The fruit should be as fresh as possible and slightly underripe, as this is when pectin is at its highest. Pectin is a natural gum-like substance in some fruits; when boiled with sugar it forms into a jelly.

The presence of acid is also essential. Acid helps extract the pectin, brightens the color, improves the flavor, and helps prevent crystallization.

All fruits do not contain the same amount of pectin and acid.

Pectin and acid are easily added to the low-pectin fruits in the form of citrus juice. You can also mix a fruit that is high in pectin, like apple, with one low in pectin, like blackberry. Commercial pectin is available, but I prefer lemon juice or to mix the fruits.

The fruit needs to become soft before the sugar is added. The process of softening breaks

FRUITS HIGH IN PECTIN AND ACID	FRUITS LOW IN PECTIN AND ACID
Cooking apples	Apricots
crab-apples	peaches
Black and red	cherries
currants	Blackberries
Gooseberries	raspberries
Grapes	mulberries
Plums, damsons	strawberries
Quinces	Pineapples
Lemons, limes	Pears
grapefruit	Melons
oranges	Passionfruit
mandarins	Tomatoes
cumquats	Squash
Guavas	Rhubarb

down the cell walls of the fruit and releases the pectin. Generally the fruit is brought gently to a boil and then allowed to simmer from 30 to 60 minutes to soften the fruit. Sometimes extra water is added to prevent burning; the amount needed depends on the water content of the fruit and the quantity in the saucepan.

Sugar

Sugar is very important because it preserves the fruit and enables it to set. It also helps to retain the natural fruit flavor and color. Too little sugar will prevent the jam from setting; too much will darken and sweeten the jam.

Use granulated, preserving or superfine sugar, as unrefined and raw sugars will smother the flavor of the fruit. Light corn syrup or honey will do this too.

Some recipes require the sugar to be warmed. To do this, put it in a baking dish, spread it out, and put the dish in a slow oven for 10 minutes. Warming enables the sugar to dissolve faster and is done when using fruits that need to be boiled for only a short time.

Try to avoid stirring the jam after the sugar has dissolved.

The golden rule for jam making is slow and long cooking to soften the fruit before adding the sugar, then very fast and short cooking as soon as the sugar has dissolved.

The Setting Point

The setting point is the exact time to finish the cooking. The jam will not set properly if it does not reach it, and if the cooking goes beyond this point, the jam will darken and crystallize. Three ways to determine the setting point:

Saucer method. Take a small saucer cold from the freezer and drop some jam onto it. As the jam cools, it should set and crinkle if you push it with your finger. Turn the plate upside-down; if jam still sticks, the setting point is reached.

Spoon method. Dip a wooden spoon into the jam, remove, and hold the spoon horizontally until the jam is slightly cooled. Turn the spoon gently; if the jam falls off in heavy flakes, it is at the setting point.

Temperature method. Use a sugar thermometer and when the jam reaches 221°F, the setting point is reached.

Bottling the Jam

As soon as the setting point is reached, remove the saucepan from the heat and remove any scum that may have formed. Allow to stand for 10 to 15 minutes so the fruit distributes evenly through the jam, then pour the jam into clean jars that have been sterilized by heating in a slow oven for 30 minutes. Make sure there are no air bubbles in the jam; dispel any with a spatula.

Air bubbles harbor bacteria. Fill the jars to the top, as the jam will shrink as it cools.

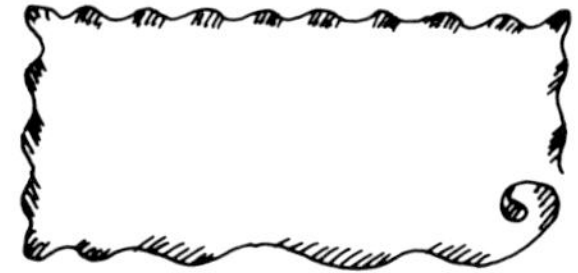

Apricot jam made from dried apricots-delicious on homemade whole wheat bread fresh from the oven.

Wipe the jars down; wipe inside the rim. Either seal straight away or cover and wait until the jam is completely cool.

Cover and seal with screw–top lids or cellophane. Moisten the cellophane when you put it on to ensure it is smooth and tight-fitting. Paraffin wax, obtainable from a pharmacy, makes an excellent seal. Melt it over a low heat and pour just enough over the jam to seal it completely. If you want to keep the jam a long time, this is the best seal. You can still put on a pretty paper or cloth cover and tie with ribbon.

Label the jam, and don't forget to date it. Store in a dark, cool, dry place.

Equipment

Use a large saucepan of stainless steel, enamel or aluminium. Never more than half-fill the saucepan, as the jam bubbles and spits near the setting point. Do not leave fruit longer than necessary in an aluminium pan.

Use only a wooden spoon to stir the jam.

Microwave Cooking

Jams and marmalades can be made very quickly in a microwave oven. I have included some recipes on page 47. The fruit cooks so much faster that it is possible to be spontaneous making jams and to experiment with different blends of fruit.

MAKING CONSERVES

IN MAKING conserves, whole fruit or large pieces are preserved and set with pectin, acid and sugar as in jam. Conserves make a lovely dessert. Follow the instructions for making jam.

MAKING FRUIT JELLIES

A GOOD fruit jelly is bright and clear and set but still a bit wobbly. The fruit taste should be noticeable. The same basic rules that apply to jam making apply here, with pectin, acid and sugar present in the right balance; but in making fruit jellies it is the strained juice from the cooked fruit that is boiled with the sugar to setting point. It is advisable to read 'Making Jam', above, before embarking on jellies.

Fruit

The most suitable fruits are apples, crab-apples, currants, gooseberries and quinces, because they are high in acid and pectin. Other berry fruits and passionfruit are delicious but not very high in pectin, so they are generally mixed with apple. The fruit should be fresh and just under-ripe. As the yield from the fruit is much less in jellies, I tend to make them out of windfalls or when fruits are reduced in price.

Wash the fruit carefully; but as the pulp is going to be strained, don't worry about removing stalks and cores and peel. The fruit is cooked in water first, the quantity depending on the water content of the fruit. Cooking is done slowly for about an hour until the fruit is very tender. In order to obtain a jelly, the fruit has to be broken down so that the acid and pectin are dissolved in the water.

Straining

The easiest method of straining is to use a jelly bag which will drip into a large bowl. They are not very expensive. The bag should be scalded before using. If you haven't a jelly bag, use a strainer lined with three layers of cheesecloth or a clean linen dish cloth and place the strainer over a large bowl. There is a third method: tie cheesecloth or a dish cloth to the legs of an upside-down stool so that when the fruit pulp is placed in the cloth it will drip into a bowl.

Adding Sugar

Measure the juice as you transfer it from the bowl to the saucepan. You will need exactly the same number of cups of sugar. The juice is slowly brought to a boil and then the sugar is added. Stir as the sugar dissolves. When it has dissolved, boil as rapidly as possible without stirring. It should take about 10 minutes to reach setting point. Use the same methods as for jam making to determine set.

Bottling

Take the saucepan from the heat as soon as the setting point is reached. Remove any scum from the surface with paper towels. Pour into warm sterilized jars immediately. Do not use large jars; small ones are best. Check for air bubbles; tilt gently to expel them. Seal while jelly is either hot or cold, not warm. Jam covers are fine for jellies. Paraffin wax is recommended for long storage. Do not move the jelly until it is completely cold or you may upset the jelling.

Store in a cool, dry, dark place, and don't forget to label and date the jars.

COOK'S NOTES: Recycle all your old bottles and jars and soak off the labels or take them off with lighter fluid. You can cover up the screw-on lid with paper or cloth tied with a ribbon. Glue the cover onto the lid. Cellophane covers always look attractive, dampen and put on hot jars to get a smooth effect. I like to make my own labels sometimes; you could copy those I have scattered through the book

MAKING MARMALADE

MAKING MARMALADE is generally much easier than making jam because citrus fruits contain plenty of acid and pectin, so you don't usually have to worry about a good set. The golden rules for jam making apply equally to making marmalade, except that the thick peel of the citrus fruit takes longer to cook than the softer fruits of jam. Read the more detailed instructions in 'Making Jam'.

The fruit should be as fresh as possible and slightly underripe; even the odd green one is fine. Scrub the skins hard to take off the wax that citrus fruit usually gets treated with to make it shiny.

To make jelly marmalade, fine shreds of peel without pith are needed. If you prefer chunky, thick marmalade, leave the pith on and cut coarsely. Always cut the fruit into the same sized pieces for even cooking.

In citrus fruits the pectin is in the seeds and pith, so when making marmalade they are usually put in a cheesecloth bag to cook with the rest of the fruit. The bag is taken out just before the sugar is added and squeezed hard to extract all pectin, which is returned to the fruit mixture.

The fruit needs to cook for a long time, up to 2 or 3 hours, to soften the peel and extract the pectin. Sometimes extra lemon juice–that is, acid–is added to ensure a good set.

As in jam, it is necessary to reach the setting point as quickly as possible after the sugar has dissolved.

Use the same setting point method as in jam making. Take the saucepan off the heat as soon as the setting point is reached. Remove scum. Allow to rest so the fruit distributes evenly through the marmalade. Pour into warm sterilized jars. Cover as for jam.

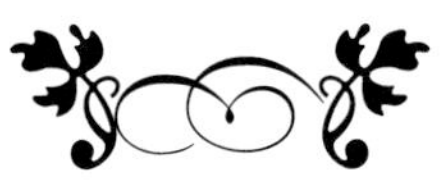

MAKING FRUIT PASTES, CHEESE & BUTTERS

FRUIT PASTE and fruit cheese are used as a sweetmeat, served with cheese or instead of cheese. They are jelly-like but dense and have a beautiful color and delicate flavor. Serve them cut into wedges on a plate. Fruit butter is usually spiced and softer and does not keep very well unless sealed with wax. Serve it as a spread for bread, scones and biscuits. Apples, quinces and damsons are the most common fruit used.

Fruit Paste & Cheese

The fruit is washed, cut up, cooked just covered in water, and simmered until very soft, then puréed in a food processor. The pulp is measured by the cupful, and the same amount of sugar is added. It is stirred until the sugar has dissolved and gently simmered for about 45 to 60 minutes. It is ready when it is very thick and a wooden spoon can be drawn across the bottom of the saucepan without there being any running liquid.

Storing paste. The purée is poured into a shallow gratin dish not more than 1-inch thick. It now needs to dry out. In hot climates it can be dried in the sun, otherwise put into a preheated slow oven 300°F for about 20 to 30 minutes, then removed and allowed to cool. Either keep it in the dish and cut off the paste as required or turn it out and cut it into long bands and then into squares. Roll these in granulated sugar and wrap them in waxed paper. Fruit paste does not need to be refrigerated. Keep it in a cool place. When serving, roll the squares in granulated sugar if liked.

Storing cheese. When the pulp reaches its required consistency, pour it into sterilized jars or moulds, label and seal. Cover and label as for jams. Serve on a plate.

Apple Butter

The fruit is simmered in the saucepan in vinegar and spices until the apples are soft and the vinegar has evaporated. The sugar is then added, and the mixture is boiled until it is very thick. Store in sterilized jars and put a wax cover on it if it is to be kept a long time. Serve in the jar.

Tomato jam is popular for lunch with my family. We generally eat it with fresh bread, a homemade pickle and some fresh fruit.

COOK'S NOTES: The pectin in citrus fruits is in the pith and seeds, so always keep them. Cook them in a cheesecloth bag with the fruit and take the bag out after the sugar has dissolved. Squeeze the bag thoroughly to extract the pectin, which should be allowed to drop back in with the fruit.

Tomato Jam
5th December

Jams

Apple & Ginger Jam

This jam is lovely with cinnamon teacake as well as spread on thick crusty bread.

3	*pounds cooking apples*
2	*cups water*
	Juice and peel of 2 lemons
1/2	*teaspoon ground ginger*
1/2	*teaspoon ground cinnamon*
3	*pounds granulated sugar*
4	*tablespoons grated fresh ginger*

Peel, core and dice the apples. The pectin in apple peel and cores is needed, so tie them up in a cheesecloth bag.

Put the diced apple, water, lemon juice and peel, ground ginger and cinnamon and the cheesecloth bag in a saucepan. Cook until the apple is tender. Add the sugar and grated ginger root, cook slowly until the sugar has dissolved. Squeeze the pectin out of the cheesecloth bag into the jam, then turn up the heat and boil very fast until the setting point is reached.

Remove the saucepan from the heat and let the jam stand for 10 minutes, then spoon it into sterilized jars. Label and seal when cool.

Apple & Blackberry Jam

This is a good way to use up blackberries that ripen so prolifically at the end of the summer. Blackberries are high in pectin.

2	*pounds blackberries, hulled*
1 1/2	*cups water*
12	*ounces cooking apples, peeled and sliced thinly*
3	*pounds granulated sugar*

Put the blackberries and half of the water in a saucepan and simmer until tender. At the same time put the apples and the rest of water into another saucepan and simmer until soft.

Now combine the blackberries and the apple along with the sugar, stirring until the sugar has dissolved. Keep the jam at a rolling boil until the setting point is reached.

Remove from heat, stand for 10 minutes, ladle jam into sterilized jars, label and cover.

Opposite: Use under-ripe Granny Smith apples for best results when making this spicy apple and ginger jam.

Dried Apricot Jam

The addition of slivered almonds gives this jam an exotic flavor of the Middle East. The jam seems to disappear as soon as I make it.

1	*pound dried apricots*
1	*quart water*
	Juice and zest of 1 lemon
4 1/2	*cups granulated sugar*
1	*cup slivered almonds*

Soak the dried apricots in the water in a bowl. Leave for 12 hours, then transfer to a saucepan with the lemon. Bring to a boil, and simmer for about 40 minutes or until tender.

Add sugar and almonds; bring to a boil, stirring frequently. When the sugar has dissolved, turn up the heat and boil rapidly for 30 minutes or until the setting point is reached.

Let the jam cool for 10 minutes, then spoon it into sterilized jars, label and cover.

Apricot Jam

This is one of the most delicious of jams. Apricot jam is my favourite way of eating apricots. This jam makes a lovely cake filling or glaze for the top of a coffee cake.

5	*pounds apricots, halved and pitted*
	Juice and zest of 1 lemon
2	*cups water*
5	*pounds superfine sugar*

Put apricots, lemon and water in a saucepan and bring to a boil, stirring from time to time. Simmer until the apricots are tender. Then add the sugar and stir until it dissolves. Turn the heat up and boil rapidly for about 30 minutes or until the setting point is reached.

Spoon the jam immediately into sterilized jars, label and cover.

Blackberry Jam

This is very good with warm bran muffins or whole wheat biscuits. It's delicious spooned over vanilla ice-cream, too.

Peel and seeds of 1 lemon
3 *pounds blackberries, hulled*
3 *tablespoons water*
2 *tablespoons lemon juice*
3 *pounds granulated sugar*

Tie lemon peel and seeds in a cheesecloth bag. Put it into a saucepan along with blackberries, water and lemon juice. Bring to a boil and simmer for 45 minutes or until the berries are cooked.

Add the sugar, stirring frequently, and as soon as it dissolves take the cheesecloth bag out and squeeze the pectin out of it into the jam. Turn up the heat and cook rapidly until the setting point is reached.

Remove from heat and allow the jam to stand for 10 minutes, then spoon it into warm sterilized jars, label and cover.

Carrot Jam

This is an adaptation of an old English recipe. It is made to imitate apricot jam, but it really is so nice it stands alone as carrot jam.

1 *pound carrots*
Peel, seeds and juice of 2 lemons
2 *tablespoons slivered almonds*
2 *cups granulated sugar*
2 *tablespoons brandy*

Wash and scrape carrots and cut them roughly. You can chop them in a food processor, but not too finely. Put the lemon peel and seeds into a cheesecloth bag. Put the carrot pulp, lemon juice, cheesecloth bag, almonds and sugar into a saucepan and bring to a boil, stirring frequently. Take out the cheesecloth bag, being sure to squeeze the pectin out into the jam. Keep up a rolling boil until the jam thickens, about 15 minutes.

Take from heat and leave to cool down for about 20 minutes, then add the brandy and mix well; this will act as a preservative. Spoon into sterilized jars, label and seal.

Cherry Jam

Vanilla sugar is made by putting several vanilla beans in a large jar of granulated, light brown or superfine sugar. Keep the lid on at all times. The beans, though expensive to buy, last for years and years. I just keep filling up the sugar levels in the bottle. My vanilla superfine sugar bottle is now 15 years old.

3 *pounds dark red cherries*
Peel and seeds of 1 lemon
1 1/2 *cups water*
2 *tablespoons lemon juice*
2 *pounds vanilla sugar*

Remove pits from the cherries and tie them up in a cheesecloth bag along with the peel and seeds of the lemon. Put the cherries into the saucepan with the cheesecloth bag, water and lemon juice. Bring to a boil, stirring frequently. Simmer until the cherries are tender, about 10 minutes. Add the vanilla sugar. Once it has dissolved, remove the cheesecloth bag, squeeze out the pectin, then boil rapidly until the setting point is reached.

Let the jam rest for 10 minutes and then pot, label and seal.

VARIATION: A few of the cherry pits can be cracked, for the kernels will give the jam a bitter almond flavor.

Carrots do not contain any pectin, so plenty of lemon was added to this carrot jam.

Fig Jam

This jam has a lovely sticky texture. It makes a marvelous dessert too; add some brandy or port to thin it, and pour over a poached pear.

2	*pounds fresh figs*
	Peel, seeds and juice of 1 lemon
1	*cup water*
1	*pound granulated sugar*

Take stalks off the figs and any skin that will come off easily. Put the lemon peel and seeds in a cheesecloth bag and place it in a saucepan with the figs, lemon juice and water. Slowly bring to a boil, stirring frequently. Simmer until the figs are soft.

Add sugar, and after it dissolves remove the cheesecloth bag, squeezing the juice into the jam. Boil a little faster until the setting point is reached. Stir frequently, this jam tends to stick.

Spoon into sterilized jars, label and store away in a dark place.

VARIATION: Use vanilla sugar for an even richer flavor.

Fig Jam
Dried Fig Jam
29/2

Dried Fig Jam

A popular jam for snacks-just pile on top of hot toast or whole wheat bread. It can be made at any time of year. The jam is dense and sticky and almost like a dessert. It can also be served in a little glass with a spoon to accompany some freshly brewed coffee.

Peel, seeds and juice of 2 lemons
2 *pounds dried figs, roughly chopped*
2 *quarts water*
1 *teaspoon fennel seeds*
3 *tablespoons pine nuts*
1/2 *cup slivered almonds*
3 *cups granulated sugar*

Soak the dried figs in 4 cups of water for several hours.

Put lemon peel and seeds into a cheesecloth bag. Place figs, remaining water, lemon juice and bag of peel and seeds in a saucepan and bring to a boil. Simmer until the figs are tender, stirring constantly.

Add fennel seed, pine nuts, slivered almonds and sugar, then stir until the sugar dissolves. Squeeze the juice out of the cheesecloth bag into the jam and discard. Boil, stirring constantly, until the setting point is reached. Ladle the jam into warm sterilized jars, cover and label.

This dried fig jam is very easy to make. It tastes delicious with ice-cream; but don't use too much, because it is very rich.

COOK'S NOTES: Pectin, acid and sugar are necessary in the right proportions in order to get a jam to set well.

Green Gooseberry Jam

As gooseberries are so full of pectin, they are ideal for making jam. They can be hard to obtain, but keep a watch out for them, as this jam is particularly good. Gooseberries are definitely worth growing if you have the right conditions.

4 *pounds gooseberries*
3 *cups water*
4 *pounds granulated sugar*

Cut stalks and tails off the gooseberries. Put the fruit into a saucepan with the water and slowly bring to a boil. Simmer until the gooseberries are very tender, then add the sugar and stir until it dissolves. Bring to a rolling boil for about 15 to 20 minutes or until the setting point is reached.

Remove from the heat and let the jam stand for 15 minutes. Ladle it into sterilized jars, label and cover.

Melon & Lemon Jam

Ginger combined with lemons and melons makes a lovely mixture for jam. Delicious with warm crusty bread.

6 *pounds sweet melon, peeled and diced*
2 *tablespoons grated ginger root*
4 *lemons, cut into thin slices*
6 *pounds granulated sugar*

Boil the melon in a large saucepan until it is tender. Drain off water and add the ginger root and lemons. Bring to a boil, stirring constantly, and add the sugar. Stir until it boils. Boil for about 20 minutes or until it thickens and the setting point is reached.

Let it cool slightly before ladling it into warm, sterilized jars. Label and seal.

Peach Jam

Peach jam is a real treat. It also makes a wonderful dessert sprinkled with chopped pistachio nuts and crumbled macaroons.

2	*lemons*
4	*pounds peaches*
4	*pounds granulated sugar*

Extract the juice from the lemons and put the chopped skins and seeds into a cheesecloth bag. Remove skin from the peaches after pouring boiling water over them to facilitate skinning. Cut them in half and remove the pits.

Cook the peaches slowly in boiling water until they are tender. Pour off all the water. Add the lemon juice, sugar and a cheesecloth bag containing skins and seeds, and bring slowly to a boil; at this point remove the cheesecloth bag. When the syrup thickens and the peaches become transparent, the setting point should be reached.

Take the saucepan off the heat and let the jam stand for 10 minutes. Ladle into hot, sterilized jars, label and seal.

Pineapple Jam

There is a nice chunky texture to this sweet jam, with a subtle bite to it that a pinch of cayenne adds.

4	*pounds chopped pineapple*
	Juice and zest of 2 lemons
3	*cups water*
4	*pounds granulated sugar*
1/4	*teaspoon cayenne*

Put the pineapple and lemon juice and zest into a saucepan with the water and bring to a boil. Simmer until the pineapple is tender, about an hour.

Add the sugar and cayenne, stirring constantly until the sugar has dissolved. Boil rapidly now for about 25 minutes or until the setting point is reached.

Take from the heat and leave for 10 minutes. Ladle into hot, sterilized jars, label and seal.

Peach & Passionfruit Jam

Passionfruit goes very well with peaches. It makes an extra special jam.

10	*passionfruit*
4	*pounds peaches*
	Juice and zest of 2 lemons
4	*pounds granulated sugar*

Extract the pulp from the passionfruit. Take the skins off the peaches after first immersing them in boiling water for several minutes.

Put the peaches into a saucepan and cover with the sugar, lemon juice and zest, and passionfruit. Slowly bring to a boil and then boil rapidly until the setting point is reached.

Take from the heat and leave for 10 minutes. Ladle into warm, sterilized jars, label and cover.

Plum Jam

Plums are very suitable for making jam, as they are rich in pectin. Plum jam can be made from small plums that are usually too tart for eating. Angelinas and blood plums are also good for jam making.

4	*pounds plums*
1	*cup water*
3	*pounds granulated sugar*

Remove the pits from the plums and put the fruit into a large saucepan with the water. Simmer until the plums are tender.

Add the sugar and stir until it has dissolved. Boil rapidly for about 10 to 20 minutes until the setting point is reached.

Take from the heat and leave for 10 minutes. Ladle into sterilized jars, label and seal.

VARIATION: Add a tablespoon of grated ginger root when adding the sugar.

Pineapple jam is translucent and has a beautiful color and texture. It is almost too good to eat.

Pumpkin 19/7
Jam
Jam
19/7
Jam
19/7

Pumpkin Jam

4 pounds pumpkin, cut into 5/8-inch cubes
2 lemons, sliced
1 quart water
4 pounds granulated sugar
2 tablespoons slivered almonds
1 teaspoon grated nutmeg

Slowly cook the pumpkin and lemons in the water until the pumpkin is tender.

Add sugar, almonds, nutmeg and bring to a boil, stirring frequently. Boil until the syrup has thickened and the setting point is reached.

Remove from the heat and let the jam rest for 10 minutes, then ladle into sterilized jars, label and cover.

COOK'S NOTES: The fruit is generally cooked slowly at first in water, the sugar being added at the end. The jam then cooks as fast as possible. This precaution will help prevent the jam from being spoiled.

COOK'S NOTES: Always allow the jam to stand for 15 minutes after removing from the heat in order to allow the fruit to distribute evenly through the jam.

Make pumpkin jam in the fall and winter when pumpkin is cheap and plentiful or your home-grown ones are ready for eating.

Redcurrant & Orange Jam

Both these fruits are rich in pectin.

2 pounds redcurrants, stalked
2 oranges, finely sliced
2 pounds granulated sugar

Put the redcurrants and orange slices into a saucepan. Bring slowly to a boil and cook gently for 10 minutes. Add the warmed sugar and bring slowly to a boil again. Boil rapidly for 7 to 10 minutes or until the setting point is reached.

Remove from the heat and let the jam stand for 15 minutes. Spoon into sterilized jars, label and seal.

Raspberry Jam

Raspberries have a marvellous flavor, and they make the most delicious jam. The jam provides a lovely filling for a sponge cake. Serve a few teaspoons in a glass as a sweet dish with coffee.

2 pounds raspberries, crushed
1 1/2 pounds granulated sugar

Combine raspberries and sugar in a saucepan and bring slowly to a boil, stirring constantly. The raspberry juice will soon begin to flow. When there is enough juice, boil rapidly until the jam is thick and the setting point is reached.

Allow to stand off the heat for 10 minutes, stir the jam once, then spoon it into sterilized jars, label and cover.

Overleaf: Ginger and orange marmalade is a nice chunky jam with a tang to it that the ginger adds. If Seville oranges are in season, use them for a more bitter than sweet marmalade.

Orange and

Rhubarb & Grapefruit Jam

This is a tasty breakfast jam with hot toast and coffee. It has a nice sharp flavor.

2 *grapefruit*
2 *pounds rhubarb, chopped*
2 *pounds granulated sugar*

Take the zest off the grapefruit, then extract the juice. Tie the remaining pith in a cheesecloth bag. Combine all the grapefruit (including the bag of pith) and rhubarb with the sugar in a bowl and leave for an hour, transfer to a saucepan and bring to a boil, stirring frequently.

When the sugar has dissolved, remove the cheesecloth bag, squeezing the pectin into the jam. Boil rapidly for about 15 minutes or until the setting point is reached.

Take the saucepan off the heat and let the jam stand for 10 minutes, then ladle into sterilized jars. Label and cover.

Tomato Jam

This jam turns into deep rich red, a really glorious color. It is lovely to eat as a lunchtime snack with warm olive bread.

6 *pounds superfine sugar*
6 *pounds tomatoes*
Juice and finely sliced peel of 2 lemons

Warm the sugar. Skin tomatoes, first pouring boiling water over them in a bowl to loosen the skins. Roughly chop them and place into a saucepan with the lemon juice and peel. Cook very slowly until the tomatoes are soft.

Add warmed sugar and stir until it has dissolved. Boil very fast for about 30 minutes or until it thickens and setting point is reached. It may take longer, as it depends on the water content of the tomatoes.

Ladle into sterilized jars, label and cover.

Rhubarb & Orange Jam

The addition of the oranges greatly improves the flavor of the rhubarb jam. Use very fresh fruit and you will be rewarded with a lovely bright color.

2 *pounds rhubarb*
3 *cups granulated sugar*
1 1/2 *cups raisins*
Juice and peel of 2 oranges
Juice and peel of 1 lemon

Wash the rhubarb and cut it into 8-inch lengths. Put it into a large saucepan, sprinkle the sugar over it, and add the raisins and the juice and grated peel of the oranges and lemon. Mix with a wooden spoon. Cover and allow to stand for 1 hour.

Bring to a boil and cook slowly, stirring frequently, for about 30 minutes.

Allow jam to cool slightly in the saucepan. Put into clean warm sterilized jars and cover at once. Do not forget to label the jars.

Strawberry & Redcurrant Jam

3 *pounds strawberries, hulled*
1 1/2 *pounds redcurrants, stalked*
3 *pounds granulated sugar*

Put the strawberries and redcurrants into a saucepan and let them cook over a low heat. Meanwhile, warm the sugar in the oven. Keep stirring fruit as the juice starts running. When fruits are cooking in their own juice, add the warmed sugar and stir until sugar is dissolved.

Bring the jam to a rolling boil, stirring frequently until it thickens and reaches the setting point. It should take 15 to 20 minutes.

Leave jam for 10 minutes off the heat before spooning it into sterilized jars. Label and seal.

A perennial favourite, strawberry jam tastes delicious with warm fresh croissants and tea.

Strawberry Jam

The lemon adds the acid and pectin.

4 pounds granulated sugar
24 pounds strawberries, hulled
Juice and zest of 2 lemons

Warm sugar in a slow oven. Put the strawberries and lemon in a saucepan and heat gently, stirring as the juice begins to flow out of the fruit. When the juice is coming to a boil, add the warmed sugar. After it has dissolved, bring jam to a rapid boil until it thickens and reaches the setting point, about 15 to 20 minutes.

Remove from heat and let stand for 15 minutes. Ladle into sterilized jars, label and seal.

CONSERVES

Cherry Conserve

4 pounds cherries
3 lemons
3 pounds 2 ounces granulated sugar

Remove the pits from the cherries. Slice the lemons finely and cut each slice into halves. Place the cherries, sugar and half the lemons in a saucepan and leave for 12 hours.

Put the saucepan on a low heat, add the zest of the lemons. When it begins to boil, turn up the heat and boil rapidly until the setting point.

Let the fruit stand for a while and then pour the warm conserve into sterilized jars. Label and seal.

Strawberry Conserve

4 pounds strawberries
Juice and finely sliced peel of 2 lemons
4 pounds granulated sugar
1 teaspoon salt

Put the strawberries in a saucepan with the lemon juice and peel, and slowly heat, stirring constantly. The juice will soon sweat out of the strawberries.

When the fruit comes to a boil, add the sugar and salt. Boil for about 15 to 20 minutes or until the setting point is reached.

Remove from heat and leave to stand for an hour, then pour into sterilized jars and cover and label.

A beautiful strawberry conserve to eat with cream.

Fig Conserve

4 pounds figs
Juice and finely sliced peel of 2 oranges
Juice and finely sliced peel of 1 lemon
3 pounds granulated sugar
2 tablespoons brandy

Place the figs, orange and lemon juice and peel and sugar in a saucepan and slowly bring to a boil. Simmer for about 15 to 30 minutes, stirring constantly, for it will be sticky. When it reaches the setting point, remove from the stove and leave to stand for 15 minutes.

Pour the brandy into it and mix gently. Spoon into sterilized jars.

Peach Conserve

4 pounds peaches
Juice and finely sliced peel of 2 lemons
3 pounds granulated sugar
2 tablespoons brandy

Skin the peaches, first pouring boiling water over them to make skinning easier. Halve and stone them and place them in a saucepan. Simmer gently in a tablespoon of water until the peaches soften. Add the lemon juice and peel and the sugar and gently stir the mixture until the sugar has dissolved. Boil rapidly for about 10 minutes.

Remove from the heat. Leave for 30 minutes, stir in the brandy, then ladle into sterilized jars. Label and seal.

Fruit Jellies

Apple Jelly

Windfall apples or crab-apples can be used for this recipe. As long as the fruit is firm and sound, it doesn't have to be the finest quality.

4 pounds apples or crab apples
Granulated sugar

Peel, core and chop the apples and put them in a saucepan with just enough water to cover them. Simmer for about an hour.

Strain the mixture through a jelly bag hanging over a large bowl or through 3 layers of clean cheesecloth sitting over a large saucepan. It will take 1 or 2 hours to strain. Do not disturb the fruit or the jelly will become cloudy.

Measure the juice; add 1 cup of sugar each 1 cup of juice. Combine in a saucepan and bring to a rapid boil. Continue until the setting point is reached.

Remove from heat, skim, and pour immediately into sterilized jars. Seal straight away while the jelly is hot. Do not move the jelly until it has finally set.

VARIATION: Add lemon peel, cloves or ginger while cooking the apples. They add a nice spicy flavor, as apples can sometimes be bland.

COOK'S NOTES: The fruit should always simmer gently in water and be very soft and mushy before it is strained. Never squeeze the jelly bag if you want a clear jelly.

Blackberry & Apple Jelly

2 pounds blackberries
1 pound cooking apples
4 tablespoons lemon juice
2 cups water
Granulated sugar

Hull the blackberries; peel, core and chop the apples. Put the fruit, lemon juice and water into a saucepan and simmer until tender.

Mash the fruit and strain it through a jelly bag or layers of cheesecloth. It will take 1 or 2 hours to strain. Do not touch the jelly bag.

Measure the juice by the cupful, and set aside the same amount of sugar. Bring the juice to a boil and continue until it thickens a little, then add the sugar. Stir well and keep boiling rapidly until the setting point is reached.

Immediately ladle into sterilized jars, seal and label. Do not disturb jars until the jelly is set.

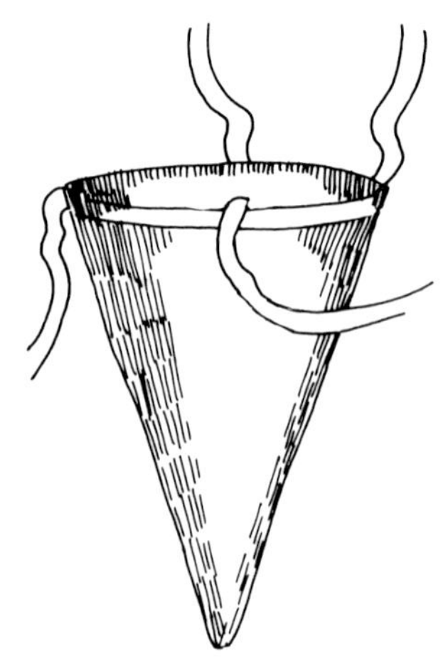

Apple & Mint Jelly

This jelly is delicious with hot lamb chops, peas and mashed parsnips.

3	*pounds green cooking apples*
	Juice and zest of 1 lemon
3	*cups water*
	A bunch of fresh mint, washed and roughly chopped
1	*cup white wine vinegar*
	Granulated sugar

Peel, core and chop the apples. Put them in a saucepan with the lemon and water, and cook slowly until the apples are tender. Add the mint and vinegar.

Simmer for 10 minutes and then drain through a jelly bag. It will take 1 or 2 hours to strain. Don't squeeze the fruit juice.

Measure the liquid in cups and add the same amount of sugar. Bring to a boil and boil rapidly until the setting point is reached.

Remove from the heat and spoon into sterilized jars immediately. A sprig of mint can be put in each jar if liked. Label and seal.

Apple and mint jelly can be used as a sauce for meats as well as a spread for bread and cakes. It has a beautiful honey color.

Mulberry Jelly

If you are lucky enough to have access to a mulberry tree, you will enjoy making this beautifully colored jelly.

2 pounds mulberries
Juice and peel of 1 lemon
2 cups water
Granulated sugar

Remove the stalks from the mulberries and put the fruit into a saucepan with the lemon and water. Bring slowly to a boil and simmer for an hour or until the berries are very soft.

Mash berries to extract all the juice. Strain through a jelly bag into a bowl. It will take 1 or 2 hours.

Measure the juice. You need the equivalent amount of sugar. Put the juice into a saucepan and bring to a boil, simmer for 10 minutes, then add the sugar. Stir frequently until the sugar has dissolved. Bring the jelly to a rolling boil and continue until the setting point is reached.

Pour immediately into sterilized jars, label and seal.

Passionfruit Jelly.

A very delicious jelly to eat with cake.

2 *pounds passionfruit*
2 *lemons*
5 *cups water*
Granulated sugar

Halve passionfruit and remove the pulp. Halve the lemons and extract the juice. Combine all the fruit (pulp, juice and skins) in a saucepan with the water. Bring slowly to a boil and simmer for about 30 minutes until the passionfruit skins are soft.

Strain the mixture through a jelly bag. It will take 1 or 2 hours to strain.

The next day, measure the liquid in cupfuls while transferring it to the saucepan. You will need the equivalent amount of sugar. Bring fruit juice to a boil in a large saucepan, then add the sugar, stirring until it dissolves. Bring the syrup to a rolling boil and continue until the setting point is reached.

Ladle immediately into sterilized jars, label and seal. Do not disturb for a day or two until the jelly is set.

Redcurrant Jelly

Redcurrants are high in pectin and make a delicious jelly which is excellent served with meats, hot or cold, and it is the basis of Cumberland sauce. I have put in some spices to add to the piquancy of this jelly.

3 *pounds redcurrants, stalked*
3 *whole cloves*
1 *cinnamon stick*
A piece of ginger root, bruised
3 *cups water*
1 *cup white wine vinegar*
6 *cups granulated sugar*

Put the currants and spices into a saucepan with the water, and simmer until the currants are soft. Strain the mixture through a jelly bag. It will take 1 or 2 hours.

Add the vinegar to the mixture and bring to a boil. Add the sugar, stirring until it dissolves, then boil rapidly until the setting point is reached – about 10 to 20 minutes.

Bottle in sterilized jars immediately, label and seal.

Quince Jelly

This jelly is a wonderful light red color. It is delicious with lamb or pork as well as on bread.

2 *pound quinces*
1 1/2 *quarts water*
Granulated sugar

Rub the furry down off the quinces and cut them up into smallish pieces. Put them into a saucepan with the water. Bring to a boil and simmer until the fruit is tender.

Opposite: Don't forgo the opportunity to make quince jelly. Its delicate taste and aroma will make all the chopping worthwhile.

Strain the juice through a jelly bag into a bowl. It will take 1 or 2 hours. The next day, measure the amount of cups the juice makes, as you will need the same amount of sugar. Put the juice back into the saucepan and slowly bring to a boil. Stir in the sugar and keep stirring until it has dissolved. Bring the jelly to a rolling boil. Boil until the setting point is reached.

Pour jelly into sterilized jars, label and seal.

VARIATION: Use apples, or crab-apples instead of quinces, following the same procedure.

MARMALADES

Apple & Ginger Marmalade

This is a jelly marmalade with fine julienne strips of ginger and lemon zest through it. It has a lovely spicy flavor and very delicate pale color.

4	*ounces ginger root*
3	*pounds cooking apples, chopped*
1 1/2	*quarts water*
	Juice and zest of 1 lemon
1	*teaspoon ground cinnamon*
3	*cups granulated sugar*

Cut ginger into julienne strips. Put it into a saucepan and cover with boiling water. Simmer for 20 minutes, then drain and refresh by placing under cold running water for 1 minute. Put the ginger in a bowl and cover with water. Leave in a cool place covered with a dish cloth for 2 hours.

Put the apples in the saucepan with the 6 cups of water and bring to a boil. Simmer for about 40 to 60 minutes until the apples are mushy. If you have a jelly bag, pour the apple into that with a bowl underneath to catch the juice. Otherwise put 3 layers of clean cheesecloth in a strainer which is set over a large bowl. Put the apple pulp into the cheesecloth and allow the juice to drip into the bowl. This will take 2 hours. Do not touch the fruit in any way or the jelly will cloud. Warm the sugar and measure the juice. If there is more than 4 1/2 cups of apple juice, put it in the saucepan and reduce to 4 1/2 cups. Now combine apple juice, lemon juice, zest, ginger and cinnamon in the saucepan. Gently heat, adding warm sugar; stir until the sugar has all dissolved. Bring to a boil and boil very fast for 15 to 20 minutes or until the setting point is reached.

Leave to stand for 15 minutes in a cool place. If there is any froth on the top, skim it off.

Spoon into sterilized jars. Label, cover and seal when cold.

Leave for 2 weeks before opening.

Cumquat Marmalade

One of the most refreshing marmalades.

2	*pounds cumquats*
	Juice and peel of 1 lemon
1	*quart water*
2	*pounds granulated sugar*

Slice the cumquats as finely as possible and remove the seeds. Put the seeds into a cheesecloth bag. Cut the lemon peel into fine julienne strips. Place the cumquats, lemon juice and peel and water in a saucepan with the bag of seeds and bring to a boil. Simmer for 1 1/2 hours or until the cumquat skins are tender. Take out the cheesecloth bag. Squeeze the bag thoroughly, allowing the remaining pectin to fall into the jam.

Add the sugar and stir until it dissolves. Bring to a rolling boil for about 25 minutes or until the setting point is reached.

Remove from the heat. Take off any scum and let the jam rest for 15 minutes before spooning it into sterilized jars. Cover immediately, label and seal when cold.

Cumquat marmalade is a favorite dish with all those who don't like their marmalades too sweet.

Ginger & Orange Marmalade

This is lovely jam for brunch parties, in sandwiches or as a filling for cakes. The muscovado sugar gives it a darker, richer color.

3	*pounds oranges*
6	*pounds muscovado sugar*
4	*tablespoons grated fresh ginger root*
2 1/4	*quarts water*

Slice the oranges finely and put the seeds into a cheesecloth bag. Warm the sugar.

Place the oranges, bag of seeds, ginger and water in a saucepan and bring gently to a boil. When the fruit is tender, add the sugar. Stir until the sugar has dissolved. Remove the cheesecloth bag and squeeze the pectin into the jam. Then boil rapidly for about 15 to 20 minutes or until the setting point is reached.

Remove from the heat and let it rest for 20 minutes. Remove any scum and spoon the marmalade into sterilized jars. Cover, label and seal when cold.

Grapefruit marmalade is made with slightly under-ripe grapefruit, with a slight greenish tint.

Grapefruit Marmalade

A nice chunky marmalade for hot toast. The grapefruit and lemon flavors harmonize excellently to make a lovely breakfast jam.

2 grapefruit
3 lemons
2 pounds granulated sugar
1 1/2 quarts water

Cut grapefruit and lemons in half and squeeze out the juice. Strain the juice into a saucepan. Take some of the thick pith off the grapefruit and put it, together with the seeds, in a cheesecloth bag. Slice the grapefruit and lemon skins. Place them in the saucepan with the fruit juice; add the bag of pith and seeds and the water.

Bring to a boil. When the peel is soft, add the sugar, stirring until dissolved. Remove the cheesecloth bag, squeezing out the pectin into the jam. Bring to a rolling boil and boil for 15 minutes or until the setting point.

Remove from the heat, take off any scum, and let the marmalade rest for 15 minutes. Pour into sterilized jars. Cover, label and then seal when cold.

Mandarin Marmalade

The whisky adds a special flavor to this jam. It is great on English muffins and also tastes excellent with cold ham or corned beef in a nice thick sandwich.

3 *pounds mandarin oranges*
1 *lemon*
2 1/4 *quarts water*
6 *pounds granulated sugar*
2 *tablespoons whisky*

Peel mandarins and cut the skin into julienne strips. Remove the seeds and put them into a cheesecloth bag. Chop the flesh. Take the peel off the lemon and cut it into fine julienne strips. Strain the juice into a saucepan. Put the seeds and pith into the cheesecloth bag.

Place mandarin strips and flesh, the lemon strips and the bag of seeds and pith in the saucepan with the lemon juice and cover with the water. Bring to a boil slowly and simmer until the fruit is tender.

Add the sugar and stir until it has dissolved. Take out the cheesecloth bag, squeezing it hard to extract the pectin. Bring the mixture to a boil and boil rapidly until the setting point is reached.

Remove from the heat. Leave the marmalade to stand for 30 minutes, stir in the whisky and spoon into sterilized jars. Label and seal when cold.

Lemon Marmalade

2 *pounds lemons*
4 *pounds granulated sugar*
3 *quarts water*

Take the peel off the lemons with a potato peeler. Cut it into julienne strips. Squeeze the juice out of the lemons and strain it into a saucepan. Save the seeds and the pith and tie them in a cheesecloth bag.

Place lemon peel, the bag of pith and seeds and the water in the saucepan with the juice and bring slowly to a boil. Simmer until the peel is tender, add the sugar, and stir until the sugar has dissolved. Remove the cheesecloth bag and squeeze it to extract the pectin. Bring to a boil and boil rapidly until setting point is reached.

Remove from the heat and allow to cool down. Stir the marmalade and spoon it into sterilized jars. Seal and label.

Lime Marmalade

A very refreshing marmalade with lovely chunks of green peel in a pretty green jelly.

2 *pounds limes*
1 1/2 *quarts water*
4 *pounds granulated sugar*

Slice limes as thinly as possible. Put the seeds in a cheesecloth bag. Place the lime slices, bag of seeds and water in a saucepan and bring slowly to a boil. Simmer until the lime slices are very tender.

Add the sugar, stirring until it has dissolved. Remove the cheesecloth bag and squeeze the pectin into the jam. Bring to a boil and boil rapidly until the setting point is reached.

Remove from the heat and leave to stand until it begins to cool. Stir the fruit once so that it is evenly distributed, and spoon the marmalade into sterilized jars. Label and seal.

Old-fashioned Marmalade

It is traditional to make this old recipe with the bitter oranges originating from Seville in Spain. They are not available all year round, so use any bitter oranges you are lucky enough to find. Sevilles tend to come into the markets in January and February, so plan ahead to make your marmalade during these months.

2 pounds Seville oranges
Juice of 1 lemon
2 quarts water
4 pounds granulated sugar

Cut oranges in half and squeeze out the juice. Strain it into a saucepan. Cut the peel finely, and put the seeds into a cheesecloth bag. Combine the juice and peel of the oranges with the lemon juice, the bag of seeds and the water in the saucepan. Bring slowly to a boil and simmer for up to 2 hours until the peel is tender.

Add the sugar and stir until it has dissolved. Take out the cheesecloth bag and squeeze the pectin back into the marmalade. Bring to a boil and boil rapidly for about 10 minutes or until the setting point is reached.

Remove from the heat, let the marmalade rest for 30 minutes, stir the fruit gently, and spoon into sterilized jars. Label and seal when cold.

Attractive tops and labels give these jars of orange marmalade a festive air. Home made preserves are always appreciated as an extra special gift.

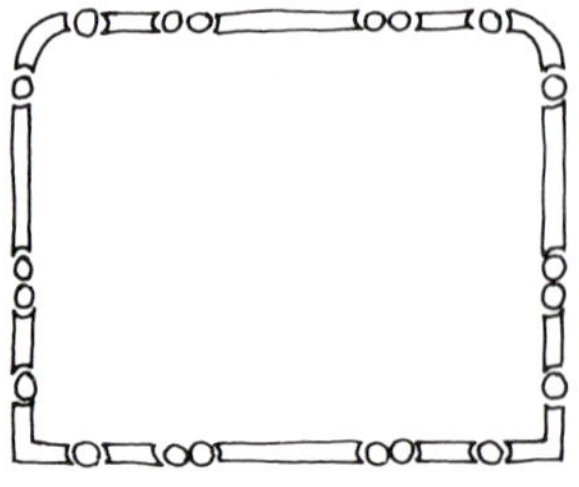

Orange Marmalade

This is a nice thick, chunky, homely sort of marmalade perfect for everyday breakfast and very easy to make. I always make a large quantity so that I have some to give away.

2 pounds oranges
1 lemon
4 pounds granulated sugar
2 1/2 quarts water

Cut oranges and lemon in half and squeeze out the juice. Keep the seeds and tie them up in a cheesecloth bag. Coarsely slice and chop the skins; do not take the pith off. Now put the orange and lemon skins, the juice, the bag of seeds and the water in a saucepan, bring slowly to a boil, and simmer for up to 2 hours until the skins are tender.

Add the sugar and stir until it dissolves.

Extract the cheesecloth bag, squeezing the juice back into the jam. Bring to a boil, and boil rapidly for 15 to 20 minutes or until the setting point is reached.

Remove from the heat and leave the marmalade to settle for a while, then ladle into sterilized jars. Label and seal when cold.

Pineapple, Grapefruit & Lime Marmalade

Pineapple is an excellent addition to the citrus fruits in this marmalade. It is a very good sandwich-filler with thick ham and chopped mint.

1	*pound pineapple*
1	*pound grapefruit*
1	*pound limes*
2 1/4	*quarts water*
6	*pounds granulated sugar*

Peel, core and cut pineapple into small chunks. Cut grapefruit and limes in half, squeeze the juice and put the seeds into a cheesecloth bag. Finely slice the grapefruit and lime skins. Place them in a saucepan with the juice, pineapple, bag of seeds and the water. Slowly bring to a boil and simmer until the fruit is very tender.

Add the sugar and stir until it dissolves. Take out the cheesecloth bag and squeeze the pectin back into the jam. Bring to a rapid boil and cook fast until the setting point is reached.

Remove from the heat and let the marmalade stand until it begins to cool. Stir once, then ladle into sterilized jars. Label and seal.

The classic three-fruit marmalade of oranges, lemons and grapefruit, served with corn bread and lemon tea for Sunday breakfast.

Quince Marmalade

Quinces have traditionally been a very popular fruit to preserve, as they have plenty of pectin. When quinces are available, it is well worth taking the opportunity of using this lovely, subtle fruit. In fact, 'marmalade' comes from the word *marmelo,* which is the Portuguese name for quince.

2 pounds quinces
2 quarts water
4 pounds granulated sugar

Peel and core the quinces and chop them into chunks. Put cores and peel into a cheesecloth bag. Place fruit, cheesecloth bag and water in a saucepan and slowly bring to a boil. Simmer for up to 1 1/2 hours or until the fruit is very soft.

Add the sugar, stirring until it has dissolved. Take out the cheesecloth bag and squeeze the pectin into the jam. Bring to a rolling boil and continue until the setting point is reached.

Remove from the heat. Take off any scum that has risen to the surface. Let the marmalade stand for 20 minutes, then ladle it into sterilized jars. Cover and seal when cold.

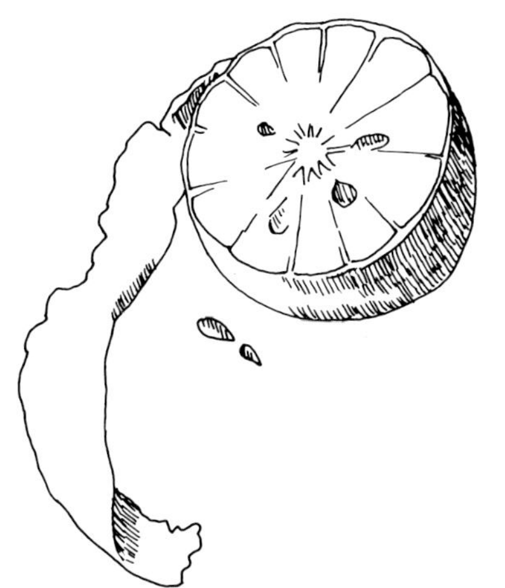

Three-Fruit Marmalade

A combination of citrus fruits makes the most popular of marmalades. There is room to experiment here – try orange, lime and grapefruit; tangerine, orange and lemon; grapefruit, mandarin and lime.

1 pound oranges
1 pound lemons
1 pound grapefruit
2 1/4 quarts water
6 pounds granulated sugar

Slice oranges and lemons finely and put the seeds into a cheesecloth bag. Remove the peel from the grapefruit with a potato peeler and cut into julienne strips. Add grapefruit pith and seeds to the cheesecloth bag. Squeeze out the grapefruit juice.

Place slices of orange and lemon, the grapefruit peel and juice, the bag of seeds and pith and the water in a saucepan. Bring slowly to a boil and simmer for about 1 1/2 hours or until the peel is tender.

Add the sugar and stir until it has dissolved. Take out the cheesecloth bag; squeeze it to allow pectin to return to the jam. Bring to a rolling boil and cook until the setting point is reached.

Remove from the heat and let it stand for about 15 minutes to distribute the peel evenly. Ladle into sterilized jars, label and seal.

COOK'S NOTES: If the jam is overboiled, the sugar will darken the jam and may cause crystallization of the fruit and also spoil the flavor. If the jam is 'runny', it could be due to underboiling or a lack of pectin or acid, or too much sugar. Try to save it by reboiling with the juice and zest of 1 or 2 lemons.

Fruit Paste, Fruit Butter & Fruit Cheese

Apple Paste

Serve this with cheese and crackers or whenever you feel like something sweet. It is very easy to make.

2 *pounds tart cooking apples*
Juice of 1 lemon
1 1/2 *pounds superfine sugar*
A few drops of Angostura Bitters

Peel and core the apples and chop roughly. Put them in a saucepan with the lemon juice and enough water to cover them. Bring to a boil and continue to boil rapidly until the apples are very soft and translucent and the water evaporated.

Put pulp through a food processor. Measure the pulp in cupfuls and add 1 cup of superfine sugar for each cup of pulp. Stir them together and leave for 2 hours, then put the apple and sugar mixture into a saucepan and boil until it has become very thick, stirring constantly. Add the Angostura Bitters, stir, then pour into a shallow ovenproof dish. It should be about 1-inch deep.

The paste has to dry out slowly. Place in a slow oven 300°F for about 30 minutes, covered. When cool, cut the paste into squares and wrap in waxed paper. Store in a cool place.

VARIATION: Instead of Angostura Bitters, add 3 whole cloves and a stick of cinnamon in a cheesecloth bag at beginning of cooking, and remove the bag when the pulp goes through the food processor.

Apple Butter

2 *pounds green cooking apples*
Juice of 1 lemon
2 *cups white wine vinegar*
1 *cinnamon stick*
3 *whole cloves*
A piece of ginger root
1 *pound granulated sugar*
2 *tablespoons rum*

Peel, core and chop the apples and place them in a saucepan with the lemon juice, vinegar, and the spices wrapped in a cheesecloth bag. Bring to a boil and cook until the apples are soft and mushy and the vinegar has evaporated.

Add sugar and stir until it has dissolved. Boil until it is a very thick mixture. Stir in the rum.

Pour into sterilized jars, label and seal.

Opposite: Apple paste being cut up and wrapped in waxed paper and tied with ribbon to give as presents. It doesn't need to be refrigerated.

COOK'S NOTES: If you are planning on giving jam as a Christmas gift, decorate the jar with some holly on the lid and red or green covers and ribbons. A red cover with a gold ribbon is very effective with a fresh flower tied in with the ribbon. One Christmas I put tartan covers on the jars with red ribbons and added a scroll of handmade paper with the recipe for the jam and suggestions for serving.

Harroset

This is a sweetmeat which is served for the Jewish Passover festivities.

1/2	*pound dates, pitted and finely chopped*
1/2	*pound raisins, finely chopped*
1	*cup water*
1	*apple, grated*
1	*teaspoon ground allspice*
1	*teaspoon ground ginger*
2	*tablespoons chopped walnuts*
1	*cup granulated sugar*

Soak dates and raisins in water for 12 hours. Put the mixture into a saucepan and bring to a boil slowly. Add grated apple, allspice, ginger, walnuts and sugar. Stir constantly, as it is very thick and sticky and will easily burn. When it is a nice thick paste, it is ready.

Pour into an shallow china dish and allow to cool. Keep stored in the dish in a cool place, covered with waxed paper.

Raspberry & Apple Cheese

2	*pounds cooking apples*
2	*pounds raspberries*
	Juice of 1 lemon
	Superfine sugar

Peel and slice the apples; hull the raspberries. Cook apples in enough water to cover them until they are soft and the water has evaporated. Add raspberries and lemon juice then cook to a pulp. Purée fruit through a food processor. Measure the amount of pulp in cupfuls; for each cup of pulp you need 1 cup of sugar. Put the fruit and sugar in the saucepan and cook, stirring until the sugar has dissolved. Bring to a rolling boil and continue until it is thick and a wooden spoon can cut across the mixture smoothly.

Pour into sterilized jars, label and seal.

Plum Gumbo

A fruit butter evolved in America. It is sweet and spicy and makes a delicious accompaniment to coffee. It can also be served with lamb and pork meats.

2	*pounds plums*
	A piece of fresh ginger root
1	*cinnamon stick*
4	*whole cloves*
1	*cup water*
2	*cups golden raisins*
2	*oranges, thinly sliced*
2	*pounds granulated sugar*

Remove the pits from the plums, then roughly chop the flesh and put it in a saucepan with the spices, tied up in cheesecloth bag, and the water. Bring to a boil and simmer until the plums are soft and the water has evaporated. Take out the cheesecloth bag.

Put plum pulp through a food processor and return it to the saucepan. Add the golden raisins, orange slices and sugar, bring to a boil and cook, stirring frequently, until the mixture is dark and thick and no running liquid remains.

Put into sterilized jars, label and seal.

Quince Paste

This is a beautiful deep red color and most subtle of the fruit pastes. It can be eaten with cream cheese as a dessert or with the cheese course. It is also very nice with meat.

2 pounds quinces
1 1/2 pounds superfine sugar
Granulated sugar

Peel and core quinces, cut them into medium-sized pieces and put them into a saucepan with just enough water to cover them. Bring to a boil and simmer until the quince pieces are soft and water has evaporated. Put them through a food processor. Measure the pulp by the cupful, and for every cup of pulp add 1 cup of sugar. Put it all in the saucepan and bring to a boil, stir frequently until the mixture is thick.

Pour the paste into a shallow ovenproof dish and dry out in a slow oven 300°F. When cool, cut into squares and wrap in waxed paper. Store in a cool place.

VARIATION: After the paste has dried, spread a layer of slivered almonds between 2 layers of the paste.

COOK'S NOTES: All equipment used in jam making should be scrupulously clean and dry. The bottles need to be sterilized and then filled either when warm or cold. Do not use tin, iron or copper spoons, skimmers or saucepan's for jams, as they can change the color and add an unpleasant flavor.

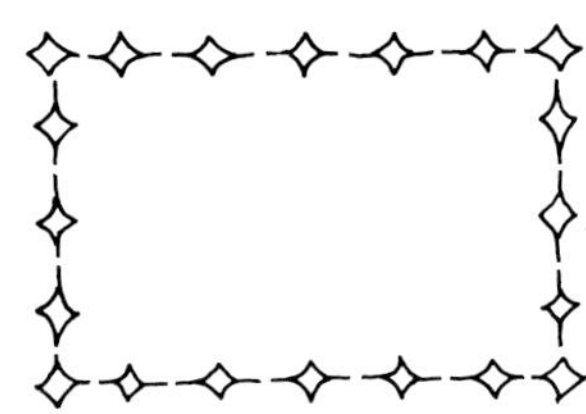

Peach Paste

2 pounds peaches
Juice of 1 lemon
1 1/2 pounds superfine sugar
Granulated sugar

Pour boiling water over the peaches and soak in a bowl for a minute until the skins come off easily. Cut the peaches in half and remove the pits. Chop peaches roughly and put them into a saucepan with the lemon juice and enough water to cover. Bring to a boil slowly and simmer until they are tender.

Add the superfine sugar and stir until it has dissolved. Bring to a boil and cook rapidly until you have a thick paste. Put the paste into flat ovenproof dishes and dry in a warm oven.

Cut into squares, sprinkle with granulated sugar and wrap in waxed paper.

Rhubarb + Orange
Jam

MICROWAVE JAMS

Strawberry Jam

A fast and easy recipe, perfect for the cook in a hurry.

1 pound strawberries, hulled
1 tablespoon lemon juice
1 1/2 cups granulated sugar

Place strawberries and lemon juice in a large bowl, at least 12-cup capacity. Cover and cook on high for 5 to 6 minutes, until soft.

Add the sugar and stir gently until dissolved. Cook on high, uncovered, for 12 to 15 minutes, until the setting point is reached; test for setting point frequently after 10 minutes.

Leave to cool slightly, then stir and pour into warm sterilized jars. Cover, seal and label.

Orange & Rhubarb Jam

3 pounds rhubarb
Grated peel and juice of 1 orange
2 pounds granulated sugar

Wash rhubarb, trim well and slice across finely. Place in a large microwave cooking bowl with the orange peel and juice. Cover and cook in the microwave oven for 16 to 20 minutes on high, until very soft.

Add sugar, remove the cover from the bowl, and continue to cook on high for 20 minutes, until the setting point is reached. Cool slightly, ladle into hot sterilized jars, seal and label.

Orange and rhubarb jam-a harmonious blend of flavors. This jam tastes lovely with pork and ham.

Three-fruit Marmalade

This is a delicious finely textured marmalade.

2 grapefruit
2 oranges
2 lemons
1 quart boiling water
4 pounds granulated sugar

Cut all fruit in half, squeeze the juice and set it aside. Remove the seeds and white pith from the peels and tie in a piece of cheesecloth. Slice the peel finely. Place the juice, peel and cheesecloth bag in a large bowl and add 1 1/4 cups of the water. Leave to stand overnight.

Remove the cheesecloth bag and add the remaining boiling water. Cover and cook on high for 20 minutes, or until the peel is soft.

Add the sugar and stir until dissolved. Cook, uncovered, on high for 25 to 35 minutes or until the setting point is reached; stir every 5 minutes and test for setting frequently after 20 minutes. Leave to stand for 15 to 20 minutes to cool slightly, then stir and pour into sterilized warmed jars. Cover, seal and label.

INDEX

Page numbers in **bold** type indicate illustrations.